Strange Majesty

The hymns of Leith Fisher

Strange Majesty

The hymns of Leith Fisher

Edited by Douglas Galbraith

Foreword by the Very Rev Dr David W. Lunan

Song lyrics © Estate of Leith Fisher
Compilation © Douglas Galbraith

Published 2018 by
Wild Goose Publications
21 Carlton Court, Glasgow G5 9JP, UK,
the publishing division of the Iona Community.
Scottish Charity No. SC003794. Limited Company Reg. No. SC096243.

ISBN 978-1-84952-592-3

Cover photo © Qiming Yao | Dreamstime.com

The publishers gratefully acknowledge the support of the Drummond Trust,
3 Pitt Terrace, Stirling FK8 2EY in producing this book.

All rights reserved. Apart from the circumstances described below relating to non-commercial use, no part of this publication may be reproduced in any form or by any means, including photocopying or any information storage or retrieval system, without written permission from the publisher.

Non-commercial use: The material in this book may be used non-commercially for worship and group work without written permission from the publisher. If photocopies of small sections are made, please make full acknowledgement of the source, and report usage to the CLA or other copyright organisation.

Douglas Galbraith has asserted his right in accordance with the Copyright, Designs and Patents Act, 1988, to be identified as the author of this work.

Overseas distribution
Australia: Willow Connection Pty Ltd, Unit 4A, 3–9 Kenneth Road, Manly Vale, NSW 2093
New Zealand: Pleroma, Higginson Street, Otane 4170, Central Hawkes Bay
Canada: Bayard Distribution, 10 Lower Spadina Ave., Suite 400, Toronto, Ontario M5V 2Z

Printed by Bell & Bain, Thornliebank, Glasgow

CONTENTS

Foreword   9

Introduction   13

The hymns:

Glory to God   16

Colours   18

Out of the flowing river   22

Come and gather round   24

Make your home in me   27

On the road   30

Come now and follow   33

Jairus   36

Man from Galilee   39

Christ is our light   42

Strange majesty   44

Colossian hymn   46

For the way your hand has led us   49

God, our gifts we lay   51

Fount of life   54

For the years of praise   57

For your generous providing   59

Voices   61

Dear Lord of every nation   64

Just as the tide   67

Holy Spirit, gracious Spirit   69

Through the city   71

Foreword

If ever a Festschrift had been published for Leith Fisher, numerous chapters would have been required to cover the range of his gifts and interests and life experiences. There would have been a chapter about his formative years in Greenock, his stable, happy childhood with his brother Jimmy, the early influence of church, the Scottish Schoolboys' Club, his love of books and music and singing, his loyalty to Morton Football Club, his encyclopaedic knowledge of shipbuilding and Clyde shipping. He could tell you not only the timetable of the paddle steamer *Jeanie Deans* – he could tell you the story of *Jeanie Deans*!

Another chapter would have to be his eleven years in the Calton area of Glasgow, employed by the Trinity College Calton Mission Society. The genesis of this project lay with the divinity students at Glasgow University who, concerned that there was no practical training in mission during their years of preparation for ministry, with the permission of the parish minister set up, funded and ran a youth club in Green Street in the East End of the city. During Leith's time there, some divinity students assisted with the different age groups in the club, but the real strength of the enterprise was the dedicated team of volunteers – up to thirty at any one time – who pioneered a new vision of service and mission in the inner city. These young people, from all walks of life, were inspired by Leith's sacrificial commitment to embody within this particular community an authentic way of bringing 'good news to the poor'. Leith never lost the perspective he gained from living and working in Calton, and he never failed to see life through the eyes of those whose lives are diminished by paucity of opportunity or by social prejudice. It was during these years that Leith met and married Nonie Macdonald, who shared in every way his faith and his ministry.

Prior to Calton, Leith had been ordained (1967) by the Church of Scotland's Presbytery of Glasgow while assistant minister at Govan Old, where the legacy and the stories of George MacLeod still lived on. He was a life-long member of the Iona Community, which George had founded. He holidayed every year on Iona, was active in Community affairs and was a key member of the local Family Group with its genius of support and accountability.

After Calton, Leith served as parish minister of Falkirk Old and St Modan's for eleven years, then of Wellington Church in Glasgow till his retirement. Throughout his ministry Leith played his part in presbytery committees and in the Councils of the General Assembly, and frequently it was to Leith that people turned when there was a situation which required particular sensitivity or measured counsel or strong leadership. There would have to be a chapter on Leith's contribution to the life of the Church of Scotland through committees, from Superintendence to compiling and contributing to the new Church Hymnary, from Christian Aid to the convenership of the committee given the daunting task of drawing up the first Presbytery Plan for Glasgow. Everyone wanted Leith on their committee, for he brought to the table a theological depth, a broad knowledge of the church and a vision of the Kingdom – not to mention his wit, his intellect and insight, and his innate ability to relate to everyone. He instinctively identified and asked 'the question behind the question'.

Chapters on his cycling, his gardening, his football prowess (where he would admit his zeal outran his skills), his regular BBC 'Thoughts for the Day', his mountains of books – he must have been the best-read minister in the Church. From the chaos of his study emerged literary creations of great beauty, deep wisdom and broad compassion. And there would be a chapter on family life with three sons and two daughters, where animated conversation covered every topic under the sun. Nonie and Leith made their home a welcome haven to everyone.

Leith's pastoral gifts were legendary. Although he was a gifted speaker, he was also a gifted listener. He gave you his full attention, his brief interventions were probing, understanding and sympathetic. His very being conveyed the presence of God, and that underneath are the everlasting arms. He was my minister and pastor during my years as Presbytery Clerk in Glasgow, and on one visit to me he asked, 'Have you discovered yet what the nature of the angel of Glasgow Presbytery is?' What would the Lord be saying to the angel of the church in Glasgow?

For all his busyness, Leith was also at his desk, sometimes late into the night, writing poems (and highly entertaining doggerel), articles, reports, letters (one of which changed the direction of my life), gospel commentaries, sermons, prayers and hymns. Each was a work of artistry – though he knew well the snare of being clever with words, and of turning preaching into mere art form. I can still hear him saying, 'Jesus did not come to give us more religion, he came to give us more life.' 'Because of Christ we are all fully paid up members of the human race.' 'Ministers are servants of the Word, and servants of the world.'

He took the leading of worship very seriously. To quote the words of the Iona Community daily office, he *'would not offer to the Lord that which cost him nothing'*. 'Woe betide us,' he once said, 'if people gather to worship on Sunday morning, and we are not prepared.' And prepared meant not only honest study, but quiet reflection on every aspect of life, and prayer. Every sermon, he would say, ends with a question mark – implying, will you go along with this? His prayers lifted us to the gates of heaven, to the throne of grace. They were addressed to God, but they spoke to our hearts. Leith's sermons and prayers would merit more than a chapter, more like a book in themselves.

The hymns Leith used for worship were always carefully selected, not only for their words and sentiment, but for their melody and mood, their key and tempo. And if sometimes there was no suitable hymn to illuminate or reenforce the lectionary texts, Leith would pen one himself for the Sunday service. It is a selection of these that, with Douglas Galbraith's skilful and sensitive editing, have found its way into this volume.

Leith knew that people might be moved by a purple passage in a sermon, or retain its overall message; they might hold on to a phrase in a prayer, or the words of a scriptural blessing – but it is what we sing that we remember. How effortlessly the words come back when we hear a melody, and what we remember is what shapes our faith. These hymns will be of value to those leading worship looking for new hymns to marry with old tunes and timeless themes, and they will be a blessing to anyone seeking to deepen their devotion to Christ, and to walk his way in the world.

David W. Lunan, former Moderator of the General Assembly of the Church of Scotland

Introduction

The fourth edition of the *Church Hymnary* (CH4) surpassed its predecessors in the proportion of hymn texts and tunes by Scottish writers and from Scottish cultural traditions. Prominent among these were seven hymns by Leith Fisher, at that point (2005) the minister of Wellington Church, Glasgow.

Leith's hymns were good examples of the new wave of Scottish writing that began with the Scottish Churches Music Consultation at Dunblane from 1961-69 (of which the late Ian M Fraser, himself a hymn writer, was instigator) and continued through the remarkable contribution to the song of the world church by the Wild Goose Resource Group of the Iona Community. The themes of Leith's seven hymns contributed to what had recently been identified as gaps in the hymn repertoire: baptism which inaugurates a journey towards Christian maturity which may begin at any age; the giving of voice to end-of-life issues; the recent recovery of the centrality of Holy Communion; and the need for hymns about the life of Jesus Christ, not least in the way this prioritised issues of justice and peace.

It is frequently the case that the published work of a successful hymn writer is but the tip of the iceberg, and this is the case with Leith Fisher. He was accustomed to write for occasions in his own congregations, to partner the scripture readings for the day or the time of the Christian Year, or to mark particular events. Before his death, it had already been suggested that more of his hymns be published and to that end he and the present editor went through each hymn marking those which were 'possible' as they stood, those which 'needed work', and those that had been significant for a particular time and place and which had now fulfilled their purpose.

Had we proceeded at that point towards publication, Leith himself would have reviewed and re-edited the texts which merited wider circulation, as he had done with those which appeared in CH4. It has fallen to the present editor to exercise this privileged function following Leith's untimely death. Where revision seemed necessary, I have attempted to second guess which scriptural passages the author had in mind and allowed them to suggest alternatives. Where a new line or verse is substituted, no notice of this is given, for they remain entirely Leith's hymns, except perhaps for 'God, our gifts we lay', where only the first verse and the Trinitarian shape have been retained. Yet there would have been no hymn without the original inspiration.

I am much indebted to the Revd Charles Robertson, who had convened the text committee which had prepared for publication those hymns of Leith's which appeared in CH4. His contribution to this book was to ensure that the editor's alterations did not stray too far from the author's intentions and to this end he made many perceptive and helpful suggestions.

It was a revelation to find how many hymns Leith had written to Hebridean melodies, often mediated through two of his favourite groups, Runrig and Capercaillie. This has led me to make use of further tunes from this rich source, along with some others from the folk tradition of the Lowlands of Scotland and beyond, or from popular composers such as Scott Skinner. However, so that hymns can be sung immediately, an alternative tune from the more common hymn repertoire has been given where the metre allows. It has been an opportunity also to tell the stories behind some of these traditional melodies, since sometimes their original themes reinforced the thrust of the hymns. It is hoped that they will bring to the collection an echo of the musical environment in which Leith wrote, together with his love of the song of the Church through the ages.

Alternative tunes are given from CH4 (*Church Hymnary: Fourth Edition*, Canterbury Press, 2005) and CH3 (*Church Hymnary: Third Edition*, Oxford University Press, 1973) but may be found in most standard hymn books.

Guitar chords have been provided for some of the melodies. They do not correspond to the keyboard arrangements and should be seen as alternative accompaniments.

Douglas Galbraith

Leith Fisher
1941–2009

16 *Strange Majesty*

GLORY TO GOD

Tune: The bleacher lass o' Kelvinhaugh (10 10 10 10)

Glory to God

Glory to God! Our living songs we raise
with all your folk of every time and place;
with saints both old and new we lift our praise
to fill with swelling sound this holy space.

Glory to God! With thankful hearts we come
for all who loved and served your people here,
for all who for the Christ made room and home,
their faith inspiring us to persevere.

Glory to God for years of service true
in church and home and in community:
the acts of grace which brought your truth to view,
the sacrifices that made others free.

Glory to God for challenges today
which call us forward into service new,
which reawaken faith and deepen prayer,
which lift our worship, and our song renew.

Glory to God! Let now our lives resound
as we step forward on the narrow road;
may you, Lord Christ, our journeying surround
and bring us safely to our home in God.

The hymn *recalls those who over time have kept vibrant the worship and witness of the congregation. Its forward-looking theme makes it suitable for a local anniversary or other turning point in the life of the church.*

'The bleacher lass o' Kelvinhaugh': *The River Kelvin runs through Leith's final parish of Wellington in the city of Glasgow, joining the River Clyde just beyond the parish boundary.* Haugh *was the name given to alluvial flatlands by a river, where in times past linen from the mills might be laid out to bleach. The song tells of the 'bleacher lass' out walking one evening, who is approached by a stranger who offers her marriage and 'fine satins braw'. She rejects him: 'I've a lad o' my ain, an' he's far awa'.' But he is that same sailor, much changed, who had embarked from the nearby Broomielaw some seven years before, and is now returned from a long voyage.*

Alternative tune: *'Woodlands' (CH4 286)*

Words: © *Leith Fisher*

Music: *Traditional, arrangement* © *Editor*

COLOURS

Tune: Null do dh' Uibhist (Irregular)

Strange Majesty

Colours

Chorus:

Lift your heart, sing for joy,
scatter dullness, banish sadness;
lift your heart, sing for joy,
welcome brightness, summon gladness.
In the colours of creation
see God's glory, see God's goodness,
and in joy and exultation lift your heart, sing aloud.

Blue the sky and blue the sea,
ever restless, never still,
sign of Spirit, living, free,
ranging through the world at will.
Green in grass and field and forest,
green in glen and furthest isle,
shows the living God is with us, present all the while.

(Chorus)

Gold the sunlight, gold the harvest,
warm and ripe and full of food;
eat and laugh and share together
and give thanks that God is good.
Brown the earth, ground of all growing,
red the blood of deeper hue,
dark the cross, the costly showing of God's love for you.

(Chorus)

See the colours dance together,
dark and bright and pale and strong,
each one setting off the other,
showing how we all belong;
in the rainbow of God's mercy
let us share the truths we know,
and in living for each other show how love can grow.

(Chorus)

'Null do dh' Uibhist': The composer of the 'Uist tramping song', John R. Bannerman from South Uist, wrote a number of well-known Gaelic songs, including 'Mairi's wedding'. He was General Superintendent of the General Post Office in Glasgow and father of John MacDonald Bannerman, the Liberal politician. Accompany the chorus in a light and staccato fashion, contrasting with the smoother style of the verses.

Words: © *Leith Fisher*

Music: *John R. Bannerman (1865-1938), arrangement © Editor*

OUT OF THE FLOWING RIVER

Tune: Oakfield (64 44)

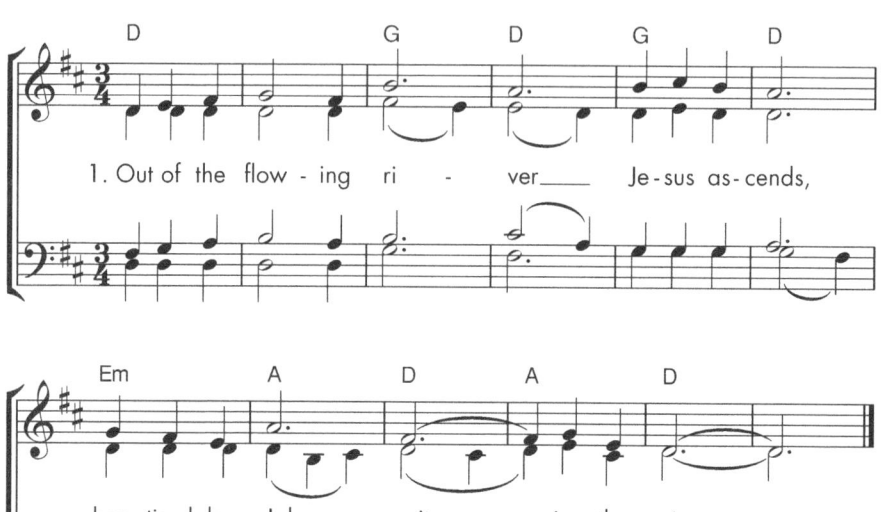

1. Out of the flow-ing ri - ver___ Je-sus as-cends, bap-tised by John,___ wait - ing the sign.___

Out of the flowing river

Out of the flowing river
Jesus ascends,
baptised by John,
waiting the sign.

Out of the open heavens
God's Spirit comes
down like a dove
in peace and power.

Out speaks the voice from heaven:
'You are my Son,
chosen and loved,
my own delight.'

Out through the life of Jesus
God's word of love,
calling in grace,
comes to our lives.

Out in the world we live in
we will make known
the love revealed
through God in Christ.

The hymn (335 in CH4) *has a simplicity and appeal to rival the once popular 'By cool Siloam's shady rill' but is suitable for baptism at any age. It is based on Matthew 3:13–17 and affirms that our baptism is grounded in the baptism and the life of Jesus himself. In his commentary on Matthew, Leith writes: 'At the outset of Jesus' ministry, we see Jesus receive from God. It is also true of us as people of faith, that we are primarily receivers. We are always receivers before we are doers, actors. Jesus' openness to God makes possible his life of faithful witness, and it is our openness to God which enables our life of faith and witness' (from* But I Say To You: Exploring the Gospel of Matthew, *Leith Fisher, St Andrew Press, 2009).*

'Oakfield' was written for these words by Timothy Redman, who at the time was organist at Wellington Parish Church. The metre is unusual and no alternative tune is readily available.

Words: © *Leith Fisher*

Music: *Timothy Redman (1943-2005)* © *Leith Fisher*

COME AND GATHER ROUND

Tune: Une jeune pucelle (86 86 88 86)

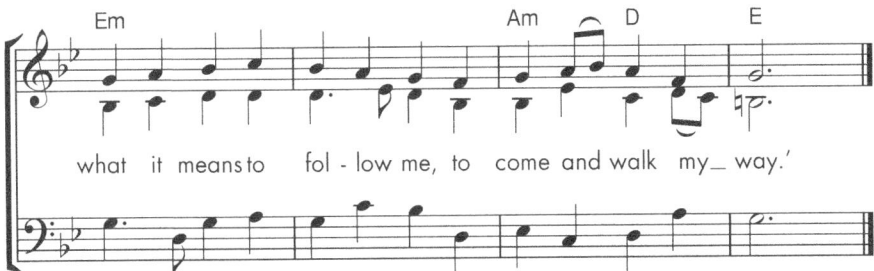

Come and gather round

Says Jesus, 'Come and gather round.
I want to teach my friends
some truths about the love I bring,
the love that never ends.
Look to the child, here in your midst,
who has so much and more to say
of what it means to follow me,
to come and walk my way.'

Christ speaks to us who, growing old,
get burdened down with care;
while caution reigns, we seldom see
God's presence everywhere.
He points to gifts that children bring –
the will to risk, the trust to dare,
through which, no matter where we are,
we'll find God always there.

When was it that we first forgot
that questions helped us grow,
or lost the openness to ask
and learn what we don't know?
Christ points to gifts that children bring –
the searching heart and lively mind
which let God's Kingdom grow in those
who seek until they find.

Lord Jesus, we have gathered round
to hear you teach your friends
the truths about the love you bring,
the love that never ends.
We look to children in our midst,
for they have much and more to say,
and join with them to follow you,
to live and walk your way.

The hymn (342 in CH4) departs from our often-sentimentalised response to Jesus' call to 'suffer the little children' (e.g. Matthew 18:1–5; 19:13–15) and challenges both church and society in terms of the value we place on children. Leith writes in his commentary: 'In our society, where so much of its life is driven by the pursuit of wealth, have we the ears to hear that it is to the "little ones", the "have nots" that the very Kingdom of heaven belongs, not in the sense of "pie in the sky" but in terms of finding and sharing the life abundant, the Kingdom life, here and now?' (from But I Say To You: Exploring the Gospel of Matthew, St Andrew Press, 2009).

'Une jeune pucelle' ('A young maid') was a French sixteenth-century carol and its tune has here been adapted to fit Leith's hymn. The same tune was later used by a Jesuit missionary in Canada to tell the Christmas story in terms familiar to the native Huron people among whom he worked, where Jesus is born in a 'lodge of broken bark', wrapped in a 'robe of rabbit skin' and visited by hunters and 'chiefs from afar'. This is a different arrangement from that in CH4, enabling it to be sung by a three-part choir.

Alternative tune: This hymn was originally written to the French carol melody 'Joys seven' (CH3 230)

Words: © Leith Fisher

Music: Traditional, adaptation and arrangement © Editor

MAKE YOUR HOME IN ME

Tune: Soraidh leis an àit (56 55)

Strange Majesty

Make your home in me

Make your home in me,
and I will live in you.
Taste and touch and see
love for ever true.

Love has come to stay
within this life of mine.
Love I give away
through this bread and wine.

Love comes from above;
I take my Father's Way,
living in his love
this and every day.

Thus I share with you
the love that lives in me.
I your life renew;
I will make you free.

I have come to tell
of joy for every heart;
joy has come to dwell,
never to depart.

This is how you prove
the love I show to you:
you each other love
just as I loved you.

The tune was Leith's own choice. The original text, 'Soraidh leis an àit' ('Farewell to the place'), was written by Màiri Mhòr nan Òrain (Big Mary of the Songs) (1821-1898). The author, also known as Mary MacPherson, was from Skeabost on Skye and wrote many songs against injustices experienced by Gaels during the Highland Clearances and since, but also songs of faith and hope. A nurse trained in Greenock, she lived for a time in Inverness and was once imprisoned for a theft she did not commit. With no language except Gaelic, she was unable to understand the procedures of the court nor to protest her innocence. The original song is now widely known, and sometimes referred to as the 'Skye anthem'. It is a lament on leaving home for exile, whether in Lowland city or far country. It should not be sung too fast.

The hymn is not about a home left but a home found. It is a simple telling of John 15, especially verses 4–13, distilling its meaning and making it memorable in metre and melody. It is also a hymn that can be used at a celebration of Holy Communion, when we 'taste and touch and see' (v.1).

Words: © Leith Fisher

Music: Traditional, arrangement © Editor

ON THE ROAD

Tune: Farewell to Fuinary (77 77)

On the road

On the road he forward goes
steadfastly to face his foes.
Dull of heart and blank of mind
see his friends hang back behind.

He's been telling them for weeks;
once more of his cross he speaks,
of his triumph now begun.
Understanding have they none.

Not in winning, not in strife,
in surrender there is life:
not in status, nor in power,
love alone will meet the hour.

Look the farce is now complete
as they fight for the best seat.
Now our Lord he has his say:
'You must take another way.

'Last is first and first is last,
all vain striving now is past;
if to me you would belong,
sing the world a different song.'

May we take the road with you,
in self-giving daily grow.
Find the gold amongst the dross –
lead us all beneath your cross.

Strange Majesty

This song *could preface or follow the reading of Mark 10:32ff (see also Matthew 20:22ff) on which it is based, or another relevant passage, or be used in the context of a sermon or prayer. It could also have a place in a Bible study group. The first five verses might be sung solo or by a choral group and the last by the wider group.*

The tune *'Farewell to Fuinary' originally belonged to a song of journeying into exile written (in English, although by a Gaelic speaker) by Rev Dr Norman MacLeod, great-grandfather of George MacLeod, founder of the Iona Community (although some attribute it to his son, minister of the Barony Church in Glasgow). MacLeod was known as 'Caraid nan Gaidheal' ('the Highlanders' Friend') for his educational and philanthropic work among Gaelic speakers. Leith's song is also about a journey, as Jesus and his disciples set off for Jerusalem.*

Alternative tune: *This hymn was originally written to 'Lauds' (CH4 616). Another suitable tune in the same metre is 'Aus der tiefe' (CH4 337).*

Words: © *Leith Fisher*

Music: *prob. traditional, arrangement © Editor*

Strange Majesty

COME NOW AND FOLLOW

Tune: The Moss o' Barradale (66 66 88)

1. Come now, and follow me. Dare to embrace the new. Come, live with me, and see; learn for yourself— it's true!— that those who risk the way I go see all around God's Kingdom grow.

Come now and follow

'Come now, and follow me.
Dare to embrace the new.
Come, live with me, and see;
learn for yourself – it's true! –
that those who risk the way I go
see all around God's Kingdom grow.

'Come now, and follow me.
The old ways leave behind.
From all disgrace you're free;
with me acceptance find
that helps you love and laugh and give,
walk straight, walk tall, and truly live.

'Come now, and follow me,
into the teeming street,
keeping as company
those no-one wants to meet.
No longer matter clan or caste:
now last is first and first is last.

'Come now, and follow me.
Push through the ugly crowd,
on to confront the fear
that motivates the proud,
empowered to cast the self away
and show the world a better way.

'Come now, and follow me.
Watch as I walk alone,
on to Gethsemane,
mount to my makeshift throne,
confront all human hate and pain
and bear all things – to rise again.'

Lord, we would follow you
into this world of now.
May we to you be true
as we again would vow
to take the road as you call 'Come',
and find in you our life and home.

The hymn in its original was so rich in theme that it expanded in the editing from five verses to six. Leith frequently explores the theme of discipleship in his hymns and here he captures the vigour, the risk, the adventure and the joy, all grounded in the life and example of Jesus Christ. The hymn can be sung by everyone together, perhaps unaccompanied, or with a percussion instrument, or the first five verses could be sung solo with all joining in on the last verse.

'The Moss o' Barradale' is a Lowland folk song which shares the 'on the road' theme of Leith's hymn, in this case tinkers travelling to a convention at the Moss. It has been adapted here to fit this text.

Alternative tunes: This hymn was originally sung to 'Little Cornard' (CH4 687). Other suitable tunes in the same metre (66 66 88) would be 'Croft's 136th' (CH4 92) and 'Christchurch' (CH4 236).

Words: © *Leith Fisher*

Music: *Traditional, adaptation and arrangement © Editor*

JAIRUS

Tune: An Còineachan (77 77 and refrain)

Jairus

Jairus, an important man, had a daughter very ill;
he to Jesus quickly ran, begging, 'Heal her if you will!
Come home and touch her, touch her, touch her.
Come home and touch her, so that she'll be well again.'

Hurried off without delay – wasn't any time to waste.
Crowds of people in their way slowed them down and curbed their haste.
Hurry to touch her, touch her, touch her.
Hurry to touch her, so that she'll be well again.

Now, a woman in the crowd – she'd been ill for twelve long years –
tired and lonely, head so bowed, weary she said through her tears:
'I'll reach and touch him, touch him, touch him.
I'll reach and touch him, so that I'll be well again.'

Secretly she bent down low, gently touched his garment's hem,
felt a strange and warming glow, knew that she was well again.
She reached and touched him, touched him, touched him.
She reached and touched him, knew that she was well again.

Jesus felt her needy hand even in that busy crowd,
called her out to come and stand; this to her he said aloud:
'Daughter, you touched me, touched me, touched me.
I'm glad you touched me; faith has made you well again.'

Jairus' daughter now is dead, neighbours wail with might and main.
Jesus calmly to them said, 'I will wake her up again.
I'll reach and touch her, touch her, touch her.
I'll reach and touch her. I will make her well again.'

Jesus took her by the hand, 'Rise, my dear,' he gently said;
'Leave your bed, beside me stand; see! your dinner table laid.'
He reached and touched her, touched her, touched her.
He reached and touched her: she was made quite well again.

Jesus, come and bless and heal all your children here today.
Faithfully we come and kneel before you, and together pray:
Reach out and touch me, touch me, touch me.
Reach out and touch me, Love that makes me whole again.

The song records the incidents described in Matthew 9:18–26, Mark 5:22–43 and Luke 8:41–56 where Jesus heals the daughter of a senior cleric and a woman with a serious condition which had resisted all treatment. In Leith's commentary on the Gospel of Matthew he emphasises how the touch of Jesus not only heals but reaches across taboos, calms fears, revives, forgives, restores. Leith writes: 'So often discipleship begins when we find that Jesus speaks to us, touches us, welcomes us, says "Yes" to us' (from But I Say To You: Exploring the Gospel of Matthew, St Andrew Press, 2009). It is a reminder that people knew Jesus physically and that there is similarly a physicality about our relationship with Christ, through our touching and being touched by others in healing and compassionate ways, or as we 'taste and touch and see' the bread and the wine, the body of Christ.

An Còineachan translates as 'The sweet little one' and is often known as the 'Fairy lullaby'. It first appeared in print in 1864 but may be much older. Leith wrote the song to this tune, to which 'Jesus loves me, this I know' had been set in CH3. The last two lines of each verse could be played more lightly.

Words: © Leith Fisher

Music: Traditional, arrangement © Editor

Strange Majesty

MAN FROM GALILEE

Tune: Kingsfold (86 86 D)

on - ly so can in you grow God's King-dom way of peace.

Man from Galilee

Who are you, man from Galilee,
disturber of our ways?
Your rent-a-crowd with shouts so loud
profanes our holy days.
Friend of the humble poor I come
to jar complacent ease,
since only so can in you grow
God's Kingdom way of peace.

How dare you, man from Galilee,
disrupt our temple trade!
Do you not care that we work here
and here our living's made?
This is a house of prayer for all
but you the truth have spurned;
so greedy fools whom money rules
must have their world upturned.

Why do you, man from Galilee,
declare our time is past?
This temple here which we revere
a thousand years will last.
Three days is all I ask to show
God's new and living home;
from death's strongroom in rock-hewn tomb
new light for all will come.

Strange Majesty   41

The why and how and who I am
all soon will be made known;
not through some fireworks in the sky
but here on earth is shown
the justice, truth and love of God
through my own willing pain.
Dying I live, and freely give
hope to the world again.

We hear you, man from Galilee,
and wonder at your way;
dispel our fear, to us draw near
since we again today
would summon courage, trust and love
to walk the road with you;
for those who dare your cross to share
will truly life renew.

The words *echo several clashes and debates in the Gospels. For most of the song, the first half of each verse captures the critical voices (in italics), to which a response is given. The two voices could be represented by dividing the congregation in two, or by having a soloist or small group represent the clamant critics, with the congregation making response. The last verse could be sung by all.*

The tune *'Kingsfold' was heard in a village of that name by the English composer Vaughan Williams and used in his* English Hymnal *(1906) for Scottish writer Horatius Bonar's 'I heard the voice of Jesus say'. It is usually thought of as an English tune but strikingly similar is the Scottish 'Gilderoy', a broadside ballad from at least the seventeenth century, and there is an Irish equivalent, 'The star of the County Down'. There is an arrangement for four-part choir in CH4, 291.*

Alternative tune: *'Vox dilecti' (CH4 408)*

Words: © *Leith Fisher*

Music: *Traditional, arrangement* © *Editor*

CHRIST IS OUR LIGHT

Highland cathedral (10 10 10 10)

1. Christ is our light! the bright and morn-ing star
covering with radiance all from near and far.
Christ, be our light, shine on, shine on, we pray,
into our hearts, into our world to-day.

Christ is our light

Christ is our light! the bright and morning star
covering with radiance all from near and far.
Christ, be our light, shine on, shine on, we pray,
into our hearts, into our world today.

Christ is our love! baptised that we may know
the love of God among us, swooping low.
Christ, be our love, bring us to turn our face
and see in you the light of heaven's embrace.

Christ is our joy! transforming wedding guest!
Through water turned to wine the feast was blessed.
Christ, be our joy; your glory let us see,
as your disciples did in Galilee.

The hymn is no.336 in CH4.

Words: © *Leith Fisher*

Music: *melody Uli Roever and Michael Korb © Hansa Musik Verlag, arrangement Compilers of CH4 © Church Hymnary Trust*

STRANGE MAJESTY

Tune: Herzliebster Jesu (11 11 11 5)

Strange majesty

Lord Jesus, as the shadows long are stealing
across your path, we turn and see you kneeling
with towel in hand, the servant way revealing,
all for our healing.

Strange majesty we find at work before us
as we, unnerved, take up the ready chorus,
'Keep back, great Lord, we rather would revere you
than be so near you.'

Yet still you come, on God's low road persisting,
from force and power so quietly desisting,
your every act upon love's way insisting.
Quell our resisting!

This hymn is no.372 in CH4. In Christ, ruler and servant were one being ('strange majesty'); it was out of his life of service that his authority came – a frequent theme in Leith's preaching and writing. Service of others is the bedrock from which the life of faith flows, but it is a truth we find hard to grasp ('Keep back, great Lord').

Words: © *Leith Fisher*

Music: *Johann Crüger,* Neues vollkömliches Gesanbuch *(1640), harmonised Johann Sebastian Bach (1685-1750)*

46 *Strange Majesty*

COLOSSIAN HYMN

Tune: Joel (87 87 D)

Colossian hymn

Christ, of God unseen the image,
born before creation's birth;
through whom all things were created,
all that live in heaven and earth –
realms and rulers, thrones, dominions,
powers great and forces small
through and for him made and fashioned –
he is in and over all.

Christ the firstborn of creation,
Christ in whom all things cohere,
all things' Maker, seen and unseen,
low and lofty, far and near.
Christ the head of his dear body,
of his Church the living core,
risen from the dead before us –
him we gladly now adore.

Christ in whom the very fullness
of the living God is found,
Christ who reconciles creation
turning earth to holy ground,
Christ the home of God's good pleasure
through whose blood is made our peace,
in whose cross, beyond all measure,
is our freedom and release.

Strange Majesty

The hymn (453 in CH4) *is a close paraphrase of Colossians 1:15–20. The passage is one of the most significant, most striking and most developed of the statements of the nature of Christ in relation to both universe and Church. Its language is 'confessional' rather than 'doctrinal', and many scholars now believe that St Paul was incorporating a very early liturgical statement, and one that was very possibly sung. To have for the first time a version which allows contemporary Christians to echo this early song of praise is the great achievement of this fine hymn text.*

The tune *is by Sally Ann Morris, who is a music director and composer in the Presbyterian Church (USA) and a visitor to Iona.*

Alternative tunes: *Among the many tunes in this metre 'Blaenwern' (CH4 468) and 'Hyfrydol' (CH4 445) might be the most suitable.*

Words: © Leith Fisher

Music: *Sally Ann Morris (b.1952) © Pilgrim Press. Used by permission.*

FOR THE WAY YOUR HAND HAS LED US

Tune: An T-Iarla Diùrach (Irregular)

For the way your hand has led us

For the way your hand has led us,
for the grace which always fed us,
here together your faithful people,
O Three-in-One, we praise you,
O Three-in-One, we praise you.

For this table spread before us
where you welcome and restore us;
here together your faithful people,
O Three-in-One, we praise you,
O Three-in-One, we praise you.

Sharing all your gifts abounding,
sure within your love surrounding,
ever, always your faithful people,
O Three-in-One, we praise you,
O Three-in-One, we praise you.

The hymn *was originally entitled 'Bicentenary grace', and it is suitable for anniversaries as well as any act of Holy Communion or another meal occasion in a local church or house group.*

The tune *is the Hebridean melody 'An T-Iarla Diùrach' ('The Bens of Jura'), a version of which appears on one of Capercaillie's albums, a group whose music Leith found inspirational. The text has been modified to suit this very fine melody.*

Alternative tune: *No alternative is offered for this unusual metre.*

Words: © *Leith Fisher*

Music: *Traditional, arrangement* © *Editor*

GOD, OUR GIFTS WE LAY

Tune: Cradle song (87 87 D)

God, our gifts we lay

God, our gifts we lay before you,
gifts of hand and heart and mind;
these we offer to adore you;
may you ever in us find
willing hands for costly giving,
spirits faithful, spirits true,
shaping in our daily living
gifts of worth to honour you.

Jesus Christ, these gifts now hallow,
differently bestowed on each,
gifts to guide or gifts to follow,
gifts to help us learn, or teach;
save us talents from exploiting,
tempted to impress or score;
use them for your Body binding,
offered to enrich the whole.

Spirit of the Son and Father,
stir the gifts we will not own,
fearful they may lead us further
into regions still unknown.
Help us love beyond our limits,
seeing Christ in all we meet;
strengthen our reluctant spirits,
make our offering complete.

The hymn *in its original version would likely have been radically edited by the author. Because the first verse and the hymn's Trinitarian structure seemed very worth saving, the editor has attempted to combine the thrust, the resonances and the insights of the original in what in effect are new second and third verses.*

'Cradle song' was written by *Scott Skinner, from Banchory-Ternan, who was a well-known fiddler and dancing master as well as a prolific popular composer. This melody should be sung at a measured pace; it could be accompanied by a solo violin.*

Alternative tune: *There are several possible tunes in this metre, but it was 'Abbot's Leigh' (CH4 615) to which it was originally sung.*

Words: © Leith Fisher, verse 1 Leith Fisher, verses 2 and 3 Douglas Galbraith

Music: James Scott Skinner (1843-1927), arrangement © Editor

FOUNT OF LIFE

Tune: Tuireadh Iain Ruaidh (87 87 D)

Strange Majesty

Fount of life

Fount of life, Eternal Now,
Source of all that's yet to be,
Maker of this earth we love,
all we sense and all we see:
from this feast of love we rise,
tuned to sing our songs of praise
of a grace so undeserved
folding us in warm embrace.

Saviour Christ, Eternal Word,
sharing our humanity,
yet within God's glory shines,
showing us another way:
from this feast of joy we rise,
knit as one, your body now,
sharing peace and bringing hope
as we in your fullness grow.

Strange Majesty

Spirit God, Eternal Breath,
wind and fire of peace and love:
teach, interpret, reconcile,
tenderly bring us to life;
from this feast of hope we rise,
swept with power to blaze God's name.
Every corner, hear the news –
nothing now can be the same!

The hymn *is suitable for following an act of Communion, or another meal occasion in a local church. However, interpreting 'feast' as a festive act, it could be sung at the close of worship.*

'Tuireadh Iain Ruaidh' (**'Lament for John Roy'**) *was taken down by Anne Macdearmid from the singing of Christine Primrose at a Gaelic song class at Sabhal Mòr Ostaig, Skye. Leith knew it from the Runrig album* Heartland *and had written another hymn to it, not one in this collection. Since the melody was clearly an inspiration to Leith, it is retained here; the metre of the words has been altered to suit.*

Alternative tunes: *'Aberystwyth' or 'Hollingside' (both at CH4 490) are suitable tunes in the same metre.*

Words: © *Leith Fisher*

Music: *Traditional, arrangement* © *Editor*

FOR THE YEARS OF PRAISE

Tune: Ar hyd y nos (84 84 88 84)

For the years of praise

For the years of praise and praying
thanks be to God.
Through each life your will obeying
thanks be to God.
For each sign of faithful growing,
every time of truthful knowing,
love for those in need outpouring,
thanks be to God.

In this house of hope and healing
our gifts we bring.
To this place of love's revealing
our gifts we bring.
Signs of thankfulness declaring,
tools for witness and for sharing,
pledge of faith, both deep and daring,
our gifts we bring.

To the tasks which lie before us,
Christ, lead us on.
Come now, quicken, nerve, restore us:
Christ, lead us on.
Freed from bonds that once controlled us,
to a truer beauty mould us,
as your arms of love enfold us,
Christ, lead us on.

The hymn was written to be sung to this tune. Its thrust is that any aspect of the life of the Christian is at its fullest and most efficacious when offered in the context of an ongoing life of thanksgiving.

Alternative tune: If a different tune is preferred, 'East Acklam' (CH4 231) would be suitable.

Words: © Leith Fisher

Music: *Traditional, arrangement* © Editor

FOR YOUR GENEROUS PROVIDING

Tune: Holy Manna (87 87 D)

1. For your generous providing which sustains us all our days,
for your Spirit here residing, we proclaim our heart-felt praise.
Through the depths of joy and sorrow, though the road be smooth or rough,
fearless we can face tomorrow for your grace will be enough.

For your generous providing

For your generous providing
which sustains us all our days,
for your Spirit here residing,
we proclaim our heartfelt praise.
Through the depths of joy and sorrow,
though the road be smooth or rough,
fearless we can face tomorrow
for your grace will be enough.

Hush our world's seductive noises
tempting us to stand alone;
save us from the siren voices
calling us to trust our own.
For those snared by earthly treasure,
lured by false security,
Jesus, true and only measure,
spring the trap to set folk free.

Round your table, through your giving,
show us how to live and pray
till your Kingdom's way of living
is the bread we share each day:
bread for us and for our neighbour,
bread for body, mind, and soul,
bread of heaven and human labour –
broken bread that makes us whole.

This hymn is no. 655 in CH4 (in the Holy Communion section), but it is also suitable for other occasions.

The tune comes from the American shape-note tradition, by which singers knew where the tune went next by the shape of the head of the note. The style was characterised by unaccompanied singing in harmony and a strong and vigorous rhythm. This new arrangement is intended to bring out the latter quality. The name of the tune, 'Holy Manna', is apt for a Communion hymn, recalling the manna which fed the people in the desert (Exodus 16:1–36), referred to in Jesus' teaching about the true bread from heaven in John 6:22–59.

Words: © *Leith Fisher*

Music: *Columbian Harmony 1825, arrangement* © *Editor*

Strange Majesty 61

VOICES

Tune: Transformation (87 87 D)

1. Poor and cold, we are out-sid-ers at your smug con-tent-ed feast; who to-day will be pro-vid-ers for my child, one of the least? Poor and cold, my child from hea-ven chose a sta-ble to be born; for your child his life was

Voices

1: Voice of the poor:

Poor and cold, we are outsiders
at your smug contented feast;
who today will be providers
for my child, one of the least?

Voice of God:

Poor and cold, my child from heaven
chose a stable to be born;
for your child his life was given
so that hope might be reborn.

2: Voice of the migrant:

War and hunger tear asunder
all the life that once we knew.
Now in no-man's-land we wander;
God, once with us, where are you?

Voice of God:

This my son was born in danger,
refugee himself became;
through him God becomes a stranger,
one with those who have no name.

3: Voice of the homeless:

Living rough in cardboard city,
this is all I call my home;
who, with kindness and with pity,
will find space to give me room?

Voice of Christ:

Homeless was I at my birthing,
as a wanderer made my way;
thus God's love did find its earthing;
I have room for you today.

4: Voice of Christ:

All who, coming to the manger,
find in me the face of God:
can't you see me in the stranger
left behind upon life's road?

Voice of the church:

Jesus, give us eyes to see you
in the last, the lost, the least;
and, in seeing you, proclaim you
Lord of love, Host of life's feast.

This song *captures a core theme in the author's life and preaching: embracing and learning from the marginalised in society and working towards reconciliation, beginning with our recognition of Christ himself 'in the last, the lost, the least' (v.4). It could be sung in conjunction with a related scripture reading or for leading into prayer. The first four lines of each verse might be sung by a solo voice or small group, the remainder by the congregation.*

Alternative tune: *'Beach spring' (CH4 252)*

Words: © Leith Fisher

Music: *John L. Bell (b.1949), © WGRG, c/o the Iona Community, Glasgow, Scotland. Reproduced by permission. www.wildgoose.scot*

DEAR LORD OF EVERY NATION

Tune: Ho ro, mo nighean donn bhòidheach (77 76 76 76)

1. Dear Lord of every nation, great Father of creation, today for our own nation we make our prayers to you. We come with glad thanksgiving for all your gifts so true; we come to pledge our living as stewards bound to you.

Dear Lord of every nation

Dear Lord of every nation,
great Father of creation,
today for our own nation
we make our prayers to you.
We come with glad thanksgiving
for all your gifts so true;
we come to pledge our living
as stewards bound to you.

For this, the land we treasure,
its beauty beyond measure,
source of our spirit's pleasure,
we bring our thanks to you.
For all our people's story –
the old that shapes the new,
both tragedy and glory,
we bring our thanks to you.

May we discern your Spirit
in all that we inherit,
as we together share it,
a common trust from you.
So, confident and caring,
as each to all is true,
with one another sharing
may you our land renew.

Help us within our borders
to lift our gaze to others,
and, one with sisters, brothers,
their hurt and pain embrace.
We pray for every nation
hostilities to cease;
we seek your new creation
where each to each speaks peace.

The hymn offers a fresh take on the 'national hymn', rooted as it is in thanksgiving for all the gifts lavished on the nation by a generous God: the natural environment, gifted people, experience from which to learn. It seeks a level of compassion and energy which is able to spill over into the global scene in the cause of peace and justice.

'Ho ro, mo nighean donn bhòidheach' ('Ho ro, my nut-brown maiden') *was translated by Professor John Stuart Blackie (1809-1895) from a Gaelic original published in Greig's* Scots Minstrelsie *(1892-1895). The hymn was written for this tune.*

Alternative tune: *No alternative is offered for this unusual metre.*

Words: © *Leith Fisher*

Music: *Traditional, arrangement* © *Editor*

Strange Majesty 67

JUST AS THE TIDE

Tune: Eventide (10 10 10 10)

1. Just as the tide creeps o-ver sil-ver sand
flood-ing the bay with slow and stea-dy gain,
like bright-ening dawn a-cross the east-ern land,
cer-tain and sure is love that comes a-gain.

Just as the tide

Just as the tide creeps over silver sand
flooding the bay with slow and steady gain,
like brightening dawn across the eastern land,
certain and sure is love that comes again.

When empty eyes stare at the vacant chair
and none can touch or fill the heart's deep pain,
into our void of desolate despair,
Jesus, pour out the love that comes again.

When every road ahead seems blocked and barred
and doubt corrodes our will like acid rain,
reveal your wounds to us whom life has scarred,
and help us see the love that lives again.

When threat and fear conspire friends to betray,
and bitter failure every hope has slain,
when broken trust makes dark the dismal day,
Jesus, speak of the love that comes again.

As sure as tide and dawn your love has come,
come to redeem our failures and our pain;
Jesus, come now, and find in us a home,
revive us with the love that comes again.

The hymn *(689 in CH4) is not just about the sorrow and loss at the death of someone close to us but about the various other kinds of 'little deaths' – loss, doubt, failure, pain – that are in their way just as powerful. The hymn cradles these within the embrace of divine love, as constant as the inexorable return of tide and dawn.*

Words: © *Leith Fisher*

Music: *William Henry Monk (1823-1889)*

HOLY SPIRIT, GRACIOUS SPIRIT

Tune: Maighdeanan na h-àirigh (87 87 88 87)

Holy Spirit, gracious Spirit

Holy Spirit, gracious Spirit, peaceful Spirit, hear our call;
Holy Spirit, lively Spirit, fiery Spirit, hear our call.
Spirit swooping, Spirit soaring, Spirit speaking, Spirit sharing,
barriers breaking, lives awaking, come right quickly, quickly come.

Empty lie our lives without you, hearts are waiting sere and bare.
Chilling winds have caused us doubt you, brought us near to grey despair.
Our dry bones come stir and moisten, rouse the lifeless into vigour
by love's way within us growing, Christ the garment that we wear.

Broken is the life among us, petty hates and fears abound;
our self-love has come between us, fallow lies the common ground.
Fire of love, come quickly, burning, melt our stubborn hearts and free us
to embrace each Christ-like other, enemies with love surround.

Alien are the lives of nations imitating Babel's tower.
Peace lies sunk in deep frustrations, justice raped by naked power.
Mighty wind of all creation, spread the seed of justice bringing
peace and reconciliation, and the dispossessed empower.

Holy Spirit, gracious Spirit, peaceful Spirit, hear our call;
Holy Spirit, lively Spirit, fiery Spirit, hear our call.
Spirit swooping, Spirit soaring, Spirit speaking, Spirit sharing,
barriers breaking, lives awaking, come right quickly, quickly come.

The tune, *to which Leith wrote this text, is from the Capercaillie album* The Blood Is Strong.
'Maighdeanan na h-àirigh' translates as 'Mary the shieling lass'.

Alternative tune: No alternative is offered for this unusual metre.

Words: © *Leith Fisher*

Music: *Traditional, arrangement © Editor*

Strange Majesty 71

THROUGH THE CITY

Tune: An ubhal as àirde (Irregular)

1. Through the ci-ty flows the stream, as clear as crys-tal, cool and clean, glis-ten-ing, spark-ling, heal-ing flood now giv-en by the Lamb of God. See, it feeds these fruit-ful trees whose

72 Strange Majesty

Through the city

Through the city flows the stream,
as clear as crystal, cool and clean,
glistening, sparkling, healing flood
now given by the Lamb of God.
See, it feeds these fruitful trees
whose leaves are dancing in the breeze,
greening revengeful hearts that brood
and peoples now seek others' good.

Come, oh come, come to the stream,
come drink the waters cool and clean;
drink from his truth and love and power
for life and strength in every hour.
Let the living Spirit flow
through all our being, as we go
forward and outward, every day,
safe on the Lamb's eternal way.

The hymn *draws on the vision beautifully captured in the early verses of the last chapter of the Bible (Revelation 22:1–7) where it is revealed to those still mired in suffering, sin and death what is surely to come: the good purpose of God will prevail and humankind and all creation will at last become reconciled within itself and with its Creator.*

The tune *to which this hymn was written was 'An ubhal as àirde', which means 'The highest apple'. It is from the Runrig album* The Cutter and the Clan *(1987), and became the first Gaelic language song to reach the UK Top 20 (1995). The music and the original song lyric were written by two members of Runrig, Rory Macdonald and Calum Macdonald. Leith would have been drawn to this tune by the way it is performed on the album, namely in the style of a Gaelic psalm.*

Alternative tune: *No alternative hymn tune was found for this unusual metre.*

Words: © *Leith Fisher*

Music: *Rory Macdonald and Calum Macdonald (Runrig), © BMG/Chrysalis, arrangement © Editor*

Copyright

Everything possible has been done to trace and contact copyright holders of material used in this book. Please notify Wild Goose Publications of any omissions or errors and the situation will be rectified at the next printing.

Books by Leith Fisher

Will You Follow Me?: Exploring the Gospel of Mark, Scottish Christian Press, 2003

The Widening Road: From Bethlehem to Emmaus: Exploring the Gospel of Luke, Scottish Christian Press, 2003

But I Say To You: Exploring the Gospel of Matthew, St Andrew Press, 2009

Wild Goose Publications is part of the Iona Community:

- An ecumenical movement of men and women from different walks of life and different traditions in the Christian church
- Committed to the gospel of Jesus Christ, and to following where that leads, even into the unknown
- Engaged together, and with people of goodwill across the world, in acting, reflecting and praying for justice, peace and the integrity of creation
- Convinced that the inclusive community we seek must be embodied in the community we practise

Together with our staff, we are responsible for:

- Our islands residential centres of Iona Abbey, the MacLeod Centre on Iona, and Camas Adventure Centre on the Ross of Mull

and in Glasgow:

- The administration of the Community
- Our work with young people
- Our publishing house, Wild Goose Publications
- Our association in the revitalising of worship with the Wild Goose Resource Group

The Iona Community was founded in Glasgow in 1938 by George MacLeod, minister, visionary and prophetic witness for peace, in the context of the poverty and despair of the Depression. Its original task of rebuilding the monastic ruins of Iona Abbey became a sign of hopeful rebuilding of community in Scotland and beyond. Today, we are about 250 Members, mostly in Britain, and 1500 Associate Members, with 1400 Friends worldwide. Together and apart, 'we follow the light we have, and pray for more light'.

For information on the Iona Community contact:
The Iona Community, 21 Carlton Court,
Glasgow G5 9JP, UK. Phone: 0141 429 7281
e-mail: admin@iona.org.uk; web: www.iona.org.uk

For enquiries about visiting Iona, please contact:
Iona Abbey, Isle of Iona, Argyll PA76 6SN, UK. Phone: 01681 700404
e-mail: ionacomm@iona.org.uk

Wild Goose Publications, the publishing house of the Iona Community established in the Celtic Christian tradition of Saint Columba, produces books, e-books, CDs and digital downloads on:

- holistic spirituality
- social justice
- political and peace issues
- healing
- innovative approaches to worship
- song in worship, including the work of the Wild Goose Resource Group
- material for meditation and reflection

For more information:

Wild Goose Publications
The Iona Community
21 Carlton Court, Glasgow, G5 9JP, UK

Tel. +44 (0)141 429 7281
e-mail: admin@ionabooks.com

or visit our website at
www.ionabooks.com
for details of all our products and online sales